IN MY little EYES

Children's Poetry

Written by Juelz Davenport

Illustrated by Zoey Wolfe

"YOUR little EYES ARE IMPORTANT!"

#IMLE

#IMLE

Copyright © 2018 Juelz Publishing

All rights reserved. This book or any portion thereof may not be reproduced or used in any manner whatsoever without the express written permission of the publisher except for the use of brief quotations in a book review.

#ISBN: 978-0-17806-5

Table Of Contents

My Raggedy Old Shoes

I Don't Care

I Can Be Anything

Dancing in the Rain

Stand Up

Basketball

Lunch Time

Buts are Yucky

The Great Big Sea

Sometimes

Birds Chirping in my Window

Trip to the Zoo

Monster in the Bathroom

Bedtime

My Raggedy Old Shoes

Wooo hooo, I'm going to race today,

as cool as the air, smooth as a cruise -- if only I had those new shoes!

I really hoped I would get some! To race wouldn't you need the right tools?

Looking down, sheesh! I am bound to lose with these raggedy old shoes!

All the children they jump, they play, blue shoes, white shoes, red shoes sooo …

cool!!! I bet if I had new shoes I could jump so high,

I bet if I had new shoes the race would never be a tie!

I would tie them so tight I would race through the light as I prepare to take flight!

I have the BB King blues due to these raggedy old shoes.

Ready, set,

Well, I guess it's time to race.

For now, these holey raggedy shoes, will be just the tool I'll use to ensure I won't lose.

One day, oh yeah, that day will come, GO!

For now, these shoes I have will have to be the reason I won.

I Don't Care

I don't care if you say howdy or wear a straw hat,

I don't care if you say what up or wear a ball cap to the back,

I don't care if you're purple, I could care less if you're pink

because we all at times forget to wash our hands in the sink.

I don't care if you're from Europe, I could care less if you're from Atlanta,

if your skin is of a dark shade or if you must go tanning.

I don't care for hate, I don't care for discrimination.

We should all work together -- we could be a great nation!

I don't care if you're plump or skinny as toothpicks,

truth is, each one of us has done a nose pick, each one of us at some point has been sick.

I don't care if your hair grows up or falls by your shoulders, because we will be dyeing every strand of gray the moment we grow older. I don't care for negative opinions; keep them far from me.

One day this world will come together -- is that too far to see?

I Can Be Anything

I can be anything

I want to reach past the stars

I can be anything

I shine brighter than any ring

I want to try harder, harder than the hardest

I want to go far, further than the farthest

I want my days to be colorful

Art to an artist

I want to be cooler than any breeze

That cool seasoned summer heat

Or cooler than the shade that lies underneath the leaf

I want to illuminate the positive and disregard the negative

Negativity I eliminate, to the top is where I navigate

Nothing but sun and days full of fun, I can be anything

I'll shine brighter than any ring.

Dancing in the Rain

As the drops drip from the cloud's midst

the sky transitions toward a grey pitch

and the sound of thunder rumbles and tumbles

and the drops get bigger from tiny to jumbo.

If you listen up I can hear them laugh through

the thud of the drops through the puddles –

splash sounds like children are proudly playing games.

I peek out the window: Children dancing in the rain,

hands in the air, drenched in the drops, hopping through

puddles like playing hopscotch, hair soaking wet,

sneakers wet to the soles, but they really don't care.

It was kind of the goal, feeling so free, it's really no strain.

There is no joy like dancing in the rain.

Stand Up

Never stand by, sit down. Stand up!

No one should be mean to anyone.

Enough is enough.

We all are unique and could only be equal,

hate is learned and can be so deceitful.

Stand up and together against anything bad.

No one has the right to make another sad.

Smiles are so cool -- spread those instead.

Being different is OK and can be so cool.

You can learn about purple even if you are blue.

You can learn about red even if you are pink.

We all look different but we all have links.

Now if you see one person being mean to another,

think of that person like he could be your brother

or she could be your sister and stand up, don't sit down.

Stand up for what's right so we can keep wrong down.

Basketball

I love to take the shots that are far, far away

I love to watch the ball as it slips away

I love watching the ball slip through the net

I love playing ball -- I want to be the best

I play when it's hot and I play when it's cold

I concentrate through the heat and shovel off the snow

I want to be captain, captain of the team

I love the game, as difficult as it seems

I love to play with friends and fellow teammates

I love the unity, I love coming together

I love playing in the gym but feel free playing in the weather

Spread my fingers and bend my knees

Flick my wrist and watch the ball leave…

Will I ever stop practicing? Not at all

Because I want to be the best the best at basketball.

Lunch Time

Sitting in class thinking about peanut butter and jelly,

all I can hear is the rumble in my belly.

I wish I could take two slices, Reese's peanut butter,

strawberry jam, dunk it in a pool of milk and lick every finger on my hand.

Breakfast was so long ago. My belly wants some lunch! Chocolate milk, iced tea and, yes, fruit punch.

Today, there is spaghetti served with meatballs.

Sauce all over my shirt.

I broke one of momma's laws.

I think I smell pudding or maybe vanilla cake --

by the end of lunch time there will be crumbs all over my face.

Pizza and fries, warm apple pies.

Then, just like that, back in class to take a test, feeling refreshed.

Lunch time is the best!

Buts are Yucky

Hey there,

there's no hay here.

No Hello,

oh!

How do you do?

I'm feeling quite blue,

Why? It is because of the things I can't do.

Who?

Me, not you!

What's the problem?

I was going to pedal my bike but, I got that feeling in my gut.

Hmmm, what's this feeling that stopped you from feeling the air breeze as you zoom …

Hmmm, I can't explain,

Well, let me explain buts are yucky!

Ha Ha Haaa,

no, really, buts are yucky! They stop possibility, they stop what could be and buts are something that I don't want to touch me!

But … ta ta ta no buts, ifs, ands or maybes -- just I can because buts tried to play me.

Let's keep buts behind us and use I cans. Now, pedal, pedal while I push.

I can woooo hoooo I can!

The Great Big Sea

How could I compare? Someone small as me.

I bet I would get lost in the great big sea.

If I put my feet at the edge,

where the waves splash ashore. I can feel the energy and

the crashing sound of a storm. I love to see the dolphins jumping in packs.

I love seeing the whales flop on their backs.

Let's deep sea dive and see the colorful fish,

the sand at the bottom -- there goes flounder fish.

I wonder if I could hear the fish underwater,

the echoes of dolphins, killer whales and orcas.

I live on the land they live in the sea; I could only imagine how deep it could be.

The colorful reef with all the crustaceans,

the shrimps, the lobsters, can't forget the crabs

with their pointy claws that reach out and grab.

It's funny you cannot see the world of the sea from the surface.

It goes deeper than the eye could see.

My imagination goes wild when I'm thinking of the great big sea

Sometimes

Sometimes I feel lonely,

sometimes things are rough,

sometimes I sit around, let headphones lift me up.

I play favored tunes, sometimes that's what it takes.

Sometimes you can tell by the frown on my face.

Sometimes I need mom, sometimes I need dad.

I really need both sometimes. That's why I'm sad.

I wish they would talk and brag about me.

Sometimes wishing is all that it will ever be.

Sometimes I'm in school and my mind drifts away

wishing and wondering for one better day.

Sometimes I feel happy, sometimes I feel sad.

Sometimes I want mom, sometimes I want dad.

Sometimes.

Birds Chirping in my Window

Sun's peeking through, it's open, I can feel the wind blow

Early morning as I wake

Birds chirping in my window

Red birds with orange beaks

Blue birds with claws as feet

Brown birds with flapping wings

Chirp chirp sing sing

Sitting side by side wing by wing.

As I sit up in bed and begin to rub my eyes

The red bird flapped his wings and took a great glide

Quickly as the red bird, the blue bird sprung

The brown bird after that the song must have been sung.

I sit in the window and wait for their return

But I'm sure they are basking in the wind blow.

I sure wish I could get close to the birds chirping in my window.

My Trip to the Zoo

The ride was kind of long -- curvy windy roads, up into the mountain

to the zoo we go. I brought along my friend so we can share this time.

My dad is so cool taking us to the zoo. We take our steps toward the cages

up on daddy's shoulders. He points at a wolf. Where? All the way up there.

We see ostriches, tall birds with long legs, bears, zebras, small birds flying around

a big bird cage. We continue to walk and right up yonder some chewing, spitting,

hairy little llamas, daddy holds me close and the llama licks my face! Yuck, ewww! Spit all

over my face! We see ducks in the pond and other types of fowl, kangaroo hopping around

carrying its child, all sorts of animals that come from the wild. Oh boy, all the walking made us hungry.

We got burgers and fries, after that a chocolate sundae. It was time to go so we all took a pic.

The zoo, yes, the zoo. It was an awesome trip!

Monster in the Bathroom

There's a monster in the bathroom.

Instead of roaring, he just flicks.

There must be flames out of his mouth.

Under the door appears to flick.

I pull the cover

over my head

because he smells like something burnt.

The flicking roars and whispers soar. I'm scared.

But no one knows, there is a monster in the bathroom.

I hope they keep the door closed.

I get the urge -- I navigate in, see the flicks of light.

I have to go -- I feel it so but I'm scared -- he's not polite.

The whispers are closer, the flicks are louder.

I turn around and just take flight.

Under the covers holding tight.

The morning should be soon.

I wish somebody knew about the monster in the bathroom.

Bed Time

Now I lay me down to sleep,

My blankets over top, underneath are my sheets.

If I should sleep past the alarm to wake,

I hope the school day they will take.

I leave open the blinds during bed time;

I stare at the stars as I travel my mind.

Never quick to sleep, always adventure

Before I drift off, headed for exciting dreams I was meant for.

There are times I hate it, last thing on my mind.

But when I am tired, I am tired! I don't mind bed time.

Are there monsters in the closet, do ghosts walk, the floor creaks?

Momma said the noise wouldn't matter if I fell fast asleep.

Moon has surfaced -- that's a definite sign.

Click on the nightlight, read a story and unwind.

Bedtime can be a great time. We all need rest.

Go to sleep early and rise with the sun.

Bedtime is great because dreaming is fun.

It's bedtime -- Goodnight!